T0045131

DEATH AT KENT STATE

HOW A PHOTOGRAPH BROUGHT THE VIETNAM WAR HOME TO AMERICA

by Michael Burgan

Content Adviser: Alan Canfora
Director, Kent May 4 Center

COMPASS POINT BOOKS
a capstone imprint

Compass Point Books are published by Capstone,
1710 Roe Crest Drive, North Mankato, Minnesota 56003
www.mycapstone.com

Editor: Catherine Neitge
Designers: Tracy Davies McCabe and Catherine Neitge
Media Researcher: Pamela Mitsakos
Library Consultant: Kathleen Baxter
Production Specialist: Kathy McColley

Image Credits
Akron Beacon Journal: Don Roese, 13; Alamy: Coaster, 53, Everett Collection
Historical, 19, 27, ZUMA Press, 11; AP Photo, 23, 52, Jeff Glidden, 58 (right); Getty
Images: Bettmann, 5, 8, 21, 29, 33, 35 (top), 41, 45, 48, 57, John Filo, cover, 17,
31, Spencer Grant, 42; Granger, NYC: ullstein bild, 24; Kent State University Libraries,
Special Collections and Archives, May 4 Collection, 7, 14, 36, 46, 59; Newscom: EPA/
Stephen Chernin, 55, Glasshouse Images, 51, KRT, 34, 35 (bottom), KRT/Lew Stamp,
58 (left), REX/Ray Stevenson, 39; Wikimedia/NARA, 56; XNR Productions, 37

Library of Congress Cataloging-in-Publication Data
Names: Burgan, Michael, author.
Title: Death at Kent State : how a photograph brought the Vietnam War home to
America / by Michael Burgan.
Description: North Mankato, Minnesota : Capstone Press, 2017. | Series: CPB grades
4-8. Captured history | Includes bibliographical references and index.
Identifiers: LCCN 2016008213| ISBN 9780756554248 (library binding) |
ISBN 9780756554262 (pbk.) | ISBN 9780756554286 (ebook (pdf))
Subjects: LCSH: Kent State Shootings, Kent, Ohio, 1970—Juvenile literature. | Kent
State University—Students—Political activity—History—20th century—Juvenile
literature. | Vietnam War, 1961-1975—Protest movements—United States—Juvenile
literature.
Classification: LCC LD4191.072 B87 2017 | DDC 378.771/37—dc23
LC record available at http://lccn.loc.gov/2016008213

TABLEOFCONTENTS

Chapter One

FOUR DAYS IN MAY

As Kent State University students went to class on the morning of May 1, 1970, some saw flyers announcing a noon rally on the campus. About 500 students out of the 19,000 at the school eventually showed up, the first of a series of events at Kent State that created shock and anger across the country.

The May 1 rally was one of many held on U.S. college campuses to protest President Richard Nixon's newest policy for waging war in Southeast Asia. Since 1964 U.S. ground troops had been fighting communist forces trying to take over South Vietnam, a U.S. ally in the region. Even earlier, the United States had sent military advisers and equipment. The advisers were not supposed to engage in combat, but many did. By early 1968, the year Nixon was elected, almost 500,000 American troops were in South Vietnam, and the number kept growing.

The U.S. soldiers were fighting the Viet Cong, from South Vietnam, and the North Vietnamese military. The communist troops received support from China and the Soviet Union. The struggle over whether the south and north would become one country was part of a larger struggle called the Cold War. Since the end of World War II, the Soviet Union had tried to spread its influence and communist

U.S. Army troops fought in Vietnam near its border with Cambodia in 1970. Nixon's plan to send troops across the border prompted widespread disapproval.

system of government around the world. The United States resisted those efforts while supporting democratic governments and trying to build a worldwide capitalist economic system.

Before his election, President Nixon had promised to end the war in Vietnam. And in April 1970 he had announced a plan to bring home 150,000 troops. But he said on April 30 that the safety of the remaining troops required sending U.S. forces and South Vietnamese troops into Cambodia, which bordered South Vietnam. From Cambodia, the North Vietnamese and Viet Cong were launching attacks on U.S. forces.

Nixon told the nation that the United States had not yet attacked the communist bases in Cambodia, which was not true. The country had carried out secret bombing raids there since 1965, and Nixon increased them after he took office in 1969. But attacking the North Vietnamese and Viet Cong bases in Cambodia would make the secret war an open one. "In cooperation with the armed forces of South Vietnam," Nixon said, "attacks are being launched this week to clean out major enemy sanctuaries on the Cambodian-Vietnam border. ... We take this action not for the purpose of expanding the war into Cambodia but for the purpose of ending the war in Vietnam and winning the just peace we all desire."

For the May 1 rally, the students gathered near a large bell on campus known as the Victory Bell. Its location on a grassy area called the Commons had become a spot for students to meet for speeches. The rally of the students who opposed the invasion of Cambodia was peaceful, but the protesters weren't afraid to show their anger. Some buried a copy of the U.S. Constitution, saying Nixon's actions had violated that document. The flyer for the rally said that "President Nixon has murdered the Constitution and made a mockery of his claim to represent law and order." The students seemed to feel that since the Constitution was "dead," it should be buried. Before the rally ended, the group agreed to return to the

Kent State University students gathered around the campus Victory Bell, where protesters buried a copy of the Constitution.

Victory Bell on Monday, May 4, for another protest.

That evening, students who stayed on campus for the weekend enjoyed one of the first warm nights of the spring. Many headed into the town of Kent, which featured a strip of bars along North Water Street. In 1970 people in Ohio who were 18 could legally drink low-alcohol beer, and those 21 and over could drink all beer and liquor. As the night went on, some young people went into the streets shouting antiwar slogans. Sensing trouble, a few members of a local motorcycle club left town after loudly racing up and down the street. Students in the bars seemed intent on drinking and having a good time. But after 11 p.m., the mood turned ugly.

Protests erupted after President Richard Nixon's TV address announcing the Cambodian invasion.

Some antiwar students set trash on fire in the street. A police officer reported seeing several people throw bottles or beer pitchers, while some people shouted, "Get out of town, pigs!" The Cambodia invasion was on the minds of at least some of the young people. About 200 students blocked the street and some asked the drivers of cars what they thought about Nixon's decision. Others chanted slogans against Nixon and the war. Some broke the windows of businesses along North Water and Main streets.

At 12:30 a.m., Kent's mayor, Leroy Satrom, declared a state of emergency. He ordered all the bars closed and set curfews for the town and the Kent State campus. People left the North Water Street bars and saw the chaos on the streets. Tear gas set off by the police filled the air. Satrom also called the office of Ohio Governor James A. Rhodes and wrongly reported that members of Students for a Democratic Society (SDS) had taken over part of his town.

SDS, which was founded in 1960, focused at first on civil rights and justice. After the start of the Vietnam War, its members began organizing antiwar rallies. Some SDS members with more radical beliefs formed a separate group called Weather Underground. The Weathermen, as they were called, were ready to use violence to change U.S. society. In 1969 several SDS members at Kent State had been arrested at a demonstration for fighting with campus police. The group lost its funding from the school after that. It was not true that SDS or the Weathermen had organized the disturbance on May 1–2. But believing the mayor's report and fearing extreme violence, an assistant to Governor Rhodes called the Ohio National Guard. Lieutenant Charles J. Barnette was soon on his way to Kent to investigate.

By the time Barnette reached the town, everything was quiet and the students were back on campus. The violence in the streets had resulted in about $5,000 worth of damage and 14 arrests. Anger over the Cambodia invasion, the curfew, and the large police presence in Kent had upset many of the young people, and a student broke a window in the Reserve Officer Training Corps (ROTC) building on campus. But on the whole, the incident seemed to be over. The next day, however, saw more protests and violence, along with the arrival of the National Guard.

In the town of Kent, merchants swept up the broken glass from the night before. Some students from the college helped. Some residents were angry about Friday's violence, and Mayor Satrom and Kent's police chief still believed radicals had stirred up the young people. The campus police chief had not received any reports that SDS or the Weathermen were at Kent State. But because the university and other colleges had been the targets of radical violence before, the idea that radicals had been at work on May 1 was hard to dispel.

Satrom did not want the antiwar students to damage property again. He banned the sale of alcohol and guns and set a new curfew that covered the time from 8 p.m. to 6 a.m. The curfew was supposed to apply to Kent State too, but the starting time on campus was later changed to 1 a.m. By early Saturday evening, Satrom also had asked the Ohio National Guard to be sent to Kent. Whether Guard troops would have any authority on the campus was not clear to officials at the school. They assumed the Guard would only patrol, if necessary, in the town, and not at Kent State. But Lieutenant Barnette had said that if the Guard was ordered into action, its troops would enforce the law both in town and at the college.

TRAINING OFFICERS

College students took part in ROTC training exercises at Camp Pendleton, California.

ROTC is the common term for the Reserve Officer Training Corps. ROTC was set up in 1916 so college students could train to become military officers while in school. The military paid for some of them to attend college, and when they graduated the officers served in the military for several years. ROTC-trained officers played an important role for the United States in World War II. During the 1960s, however, as the protests against the Vietnam War grew, some students directed their anger against the ROTC programs at their schools. Some universities decided to end their programs. In the years after the war, ROTC began to grow again, especially as the military tried to recruit women and African-Americans to become officers. The September 11, 2001, terrorist attacks on the United States also helped ROTC, as more young Americans took pride in joining the military. Today more than 1,000 colleges have ROTC programs.

Students on campus heard about the curfew in town, and some made plans to go to dances at the school that had been quickly organized to entertain them. Students opposed to the war, however, sent out word that there would be a rally that night at the Victory Bell. School officials had told students they could meet publicly if they remained peaceful. By 7:30 pm., about 600 students were gathered around the bell. Many spread around the campus to find more students to join them, and the crowd grew to about 1,000.

Some of the protesters clearly did not want to just talk about Cambodia and the larger war. They wanted to take action. They headed toward the ROTC building, which to them seemed to represent everything bad about the war and the U.S. military. A few people shouted "Get it!" and "Burn it!" while some protesters threw rocks at the building. A few threw lit flares through open windows, hoping to start a fire. The flares didn't catch, but other students kept trying to ignite a fire, and by 8:45 the building was burning.

Kent Fire Department firefighters arrived and put the fire out, while some protesters threw stones or otherwise tried to stop their efforts. Around 9:45 p.m., though, another fire started. The firefighters returned, this time with local police protection. Minutes later hundreds of Ohio National Guard troops arrived. To Ruth Gibson, a Kent State student, the arrival of the troops seemed like something out of a movie.

School officials had told students they could meet publicly if they remained peaceful.

National Guard troops were on hand after the ROTC building burst into flames a second time.

"I had to keep reminding myself that everything that had happened was real," she said later. With their bayonets fixed on their rifles and using tear gas, the guardsmen forced the students out of the Commons and into dorms. Students and officials once again debated whether non-student radicals had first called for burning the ROTC building. Most of the students who came out that night merely watched the violence and did not take part.

When Kent State students woke up on Sunday, May 3, there were 850 guardsmen on the campus, along with their trucks, jeeps, and armored vehicles. The units had just spent several days in Akron, Ohio, trying to stop violence related to a strike by truck

The rifles issued to the National Guardsmen on campus had bayonets and live ammunition.

drivers. The guardsmen were tired, and most had probably hoped to be on their way home, instead of dealing with trouble at Kent State.

Governor Rhodes came into Kent at 10 a.m. He met with local officials and saw the heavily damaged ROTC building. Rhodes assured citizens that he would take tough action against the most radical protesters. He called them "the worst type of people that we harbor in America," and he vowed that "they are not going to take over the campus." While some county officials thought Rhodes should close the campus to let emotions cool, Rhodes said no. He thought that would just be giving in to the radicals.

After the burning of the ROTC building, officials banned all public rallies in Kent, but students ignored the ban and once again gathered at the Victory Bell. Now many were protesting the presence of the National Guard on campus.

The curfew was changed to 9 p.m., but as that hour came the students refused to leave the Commons. Police once again broke up the crowd with tear gas. Around 10 p.m. several hundred students sat in the streets to shut down traffic. They wanted to present a list of demands to Mayor Satrom and school officials. One student talked to police and thought they had agreed that the National Guard would leave the campus.

Instead, the guardsmen broke up the demonstration. When some students pelted them with rocks, the troops responded with tear gas, and some bayoneted students. The students sought safety in campus buildings. Some climbed through the open windows of the library to escape the guardsmen, who swung their rifle butts at any protester who was close to them. A helicopter hovered over the campus, shining searchlights on the action below.

As classes began on Monday, May 4, the National Guard was still on the campus. Some soldiers guarded the entrances to the school while others watched over the ruined ROTC building. City and university officials met with the National Guard's

General Robert Canterbury to discuss the situation. They assumed that the rally planned for noon would not be allowed. But at 11 a.m., when someone began to ring the Victory Bell, students gathered at the Commons. Once again, some came as much to protest the Guard presence at Kent State as the war in Vietnam. By 11:45 a.m., several thousand students were on or near the Commons. Some shouted slogans, while a larger group watched from a nearby hill.

A Kent State police officer rode in a National Guard jeep, telling the crowd to leave. He was greeted with angry shouts and rocks. General Canterbury had ordered his men to load their rifles, and some fired tear gas grenades. Soon 76 armed guardsmen were ordered to march toward the crowd. Some students threw grenades back at the troops, while others threw rocks. Many of the students later said they felt that the ban on the rally and the Guard's presence had trampled their rights. They were not in a mood to back down.

At one point some guardsmen were ordered to kneel and aim at the students, but they did not shoot. The guardsmen then retreated toward the Commons. A small group of students followed the retreating guardsmen. Then, at 12:24 p.m., the guardsmen reached the top of a hill. About 12 of them turned and opened fire. In just under 13 seconds, they fired 67 shots.

In just under 13 seconds, they fired 67 shots.

The photo of Mary Ann Vecchio crying over the body of Jeffrey Miller would become a symbol of the antiwar movement.

Students ran or dived for cover, but some of the bullets found their targets. In those few seconds, the guardsmen hit 13 students. One of them was Jeffrey Miller, who was in a parking lot about 270 feet (82 meters) away from the shooters. Miller fell to the pavement, dead. In an instant, a young woman, Mary Ann Vecchio, was kneeling over his body, calling for help. Standing nearby was John Filo, who was studying photojournalism at Kent State. He snapped a picture that captured the anguish of the day and, some believed, of the Vietnam War.

Chapter Two

THE PATH TO KENT STATE

The killings on May 4, 1970, happened during a foreign war with deep roots. It was also a war that, over time, a growing number of Americans did not want the United States to fight.

At the end of World War II, Vietnam was not an independent country, though it once had been. In 1945 Vietnam was part of a French colony called Indochina, which included Cambodia and Laos. French missionaries had come to the region in the 1600s seeking to convert the local people to the Roman Catholic faith. Later the French government promoted trade with Indochina. By the end of the 1800s, after several decades of warfare, France had taken control of the region.

During World War II, Indochina came under Japanese control after France was invaded by Germany. Nationalists such as Ho Chi Minh fought the Japanese and aided the Allies, which included France and the United States. Ho led the Viet Minh, a group that wanted Vietnamese independence. During the war Ho worked with the U.S. Office of Strategic Services, which served as the model for today's Central Intelligence Agency. The Viet Minh helped rescue downed American pilots.

After Japan's surrender in September 1945,

Ho Chi Minh posed with two girls in 1954. Ho led the Vietnamese nationalist movement for more than 30 years, first against the Japanese, then the French, and then the U.S.-backed South Vietnamese.

Ho proclaimed Vietnam's independence. France, though, wanted its old colony back. It agreed to give Vietnam some control over its affairs but not as much as Ho and the Viet Minh wanted. At the end of 1946, the two sides began battling to see who would control Vietnam's future. A few years later, France set up a separate government in the south that accepted some French control. Ho remained firmly in control in the north.

Despite working with Ho during World War II, the U.S. government did not recognize him as the leader of an independent Vietnam. It backed the new southern government because Ho was a communist as well as a nationalist. As the war with France went on, the communist governments in China and the Soviet Union recognized Ho as the rightful leader of all of Vietnam. The Chinese also sent military supplies. The United States gave France aid to fight the communists.

President Harry Truman and later presidents saw the conflict in Vietnam as part of the Cold War. In 1954, President Dwight D. Eisenhower compared Vietnam and its neighbors to dominoes. If Vietnam fell under communist rule, the thinking went, other countries in the region would be more likely to fall too. Referring to China's becoming communist in 1949, Eisenhower said, "Asia, after all, has already lost some 450 million of its peoples to the Communist dictatorship, and we simply can't afford greater losses."

Ho and the Viet Minh, however, defeated France in 1954. Vietnam won its independence, but kept two separate governments—communist North Vietnam and democratic South Vietnam. The south was basically democratic in name only. Most of its rulers were corrupt, seeking to preserve their own power and build wealth for their families. Meanwhile, Ho

President Lyndon Johnson would dramatically increase the number of troops fighting in Vietnam.

still wanted to unite the country under his rule. His government armed and trained communist fighters in the south, the Viet Cong, while South Vietnam received aid from the United States to battle its enemies.

Under President John F. Kennedy, the number of U.S. soldiers in South Vietnam grew. Shortly after Kennedy's assassination in 1963, the number of military advisers was just over 16,000. Over the next year, the new president, Lyndon Johnson, sent 7,000 more, and in February 1965, U.S. warplanes began a sustained assault on North Vietnam. In March

Johnson sent more combat troops into South Vietnam. The war had entered a new phase, and the number of Americans fighting in Southeast Asia would rise dramatically over the next four years.

In the months after the ground troops went to Vietnam, most Americans seemed to favor the U.S. military action there. But almost from the start the war had some vocal critics in the United States. The antiwar movement included pacifists, who opposed all wars, as well as people who thought the money being spent in Vietnam could be put to better use in the United States. Other antiwar activists thought the United States was killing Vietnamese who weren't soldiers and sending its own young men off to die for no good reason. They did not see North Vietnam as a threat, despite Eisenhower's domino theory. Many thought the war was ill-conceived and doomed to fail. Others worried about its effect on the U.S. reputation abroad. In addition, young men faced the risk of being drafted into the army. Many of them did not want to fight and possibly die in a war, especially one they did not support.

One of the first major antiwar protests took place in Washington, D.C., in April 1965. SDS and other antiwar groups organized the event, which drew about 16,000 people. In October, people across the country took part in the International Days of Protest. It was illegal to destroy draft cards, but that didn't stop many young men from publicly

But almost from the start the war had some vocal critics in the United States.

Demonstrators in support of the Vietnam War marched near the White House in April 1965. Antiwar protesters also filled the streets of Washington that month.

burning their cards to show their opposition to the war. In Boston, about 3,000 people took part in the October protests. A newspaper opinion article in Boston warned that most of the protesters, or at least the events' organizers, were communists. Antiwar activists continued to face the charge that they were unpatriotic, if not communist. Young people who supported the war also came out in Boston, holding signs that called for bombing Vietnam. One said, "Send the Draft Dodgers to Viet Nam."

Over the next few years, as more U.S. troops went to Vietnam and the number of casualties grew, the size of the protests increased dramatically.

A massive parade of protesters marched past the United Nations building in New York City on April 15, 1967.

On April 15, 1967, more than 100,000 protesters turned out in New York City. The month before, Martin Luther King Jr. led 5,000 protesters through downtown Chicago. King was one of the leaders of the civil rights movement, fighting to win equality for African-Americans. He had come to see the Vietnam War as another major problem for the country. The war took attention away from problems at home, including civil rights. "We arm Negro soldiers to kill on foreign battlefields," King said, "but offer little protection for their relatives from beatings and killings in our own South."

At some protests, hundreds of men burned their draft cards while thousands of people watched. At times, the police sent huge numbers of officers to the rallies. At a June 1967 protest in Los Angeles, about 1,300 police showed up to keep order at a protest that drew 10,000 people into the streets. The police ordered them to leave, but the crowd refused. Hundreds of officers rushed the protesters with nightsticks, injuring dozens.

Radical protesters welcomed clashes with the police. They did not think peaceful protests would end the war or bring other changes to society. To the radicals, the war was the product of a system that did not value minorities, the young, and the poor. But many antiwar protesters were not radical. They wanted to peacefully protest to try to end the Vietnam War as soon as possible. Still, even more violence erupted in Chicago the next year, when the Democratic Party met there to choose its candidate for the 1968 presidential election. The police beat protesters, and even bystanders, as they tried to clear the city's streets and parks.

Despite the large protests, many Americans said they supported Johnson's efforts to fight communism in Southeast Asia. But that support fell as the number of casualties kept rising. By the time Richard Nixon took office in January 1969, surveys showed that just over half of Americans opposed the war, compared with about one-third who supported it. More than 30,000 Americans had died in the fighting since the late 1950s.

Nixon ran for president promising Americans that his main goal would be to end the war. Once in office, he began a policy called Vietnamization. He would pull out U.S. troops as South Vietnamese troops did more of the fighting. Even with that policy, more than 10,000 additional Americans were killed during Nixon's first year in office. He realized that his approach to the war was not healing the divisions in the country, and that some people believed the government had not been telling them the truth about Vietnam for most of the war.

Nixon addressed the nation on November 3, 1969, trying to answer some of the concerns Americans had about the war. He explained the Cold War context that led to U.S. involvement and said he wanted a peace deal that would protect non-Communists in the south. He mentioned the ongoing peace talks in Paris and his orders to withdraw U.S. troops. But pulling out completely and immediately, he argued, was not possible. "For the United States," he said, "this first defeat in our Nation's history would result in a collapse of confidence in American leadership, not only in Asia but throughout the world."

Nixon also addressed what he called "the silent majority"—Americans who agreed that a defeat in Vietnam would be awful for the country and for

"For the United States, this first defeat in our Nation's history would result in a collapse of confidence in American leadership, not only in Asia but throughout the world."

Protesters expressed their antiwar sentiments by burning little American flags.

South Vietnam. The silent majority did not support the students and others who protested against the war. Nixon called on Americans to end their divisions over the war and support his efforts. He said, "The more support I can have from the American people, the sooner that pledge [to end the war] can be redeemed; for the more divided we are at home, the less likely the enemy is to negotiate at Paris."

The speech struck a nerve with many Americans. Nixon received 80,000 letters and telegrams after it, and most of them expressed approval of what he said. But the speech did little to change the minds of the young and the antiwar activists. On November 13, about 45,000 people marched through Washington and past the White House. Each held a sign with the name of someone who had died during the war or the name of a Vietnamese village destroyed during the fighting. As they passed the White House, the marchers called out the names written on the signs.

Then, on November 15, protesters held the largest antiwar demonstration in American history. As many as half a million people turned out for what *The New York Times* called a "great and peaceful army of dissent moving through the city." The day, though, was not completely peaceful. After the rally, small numbers of radicals burned American flags and threw paint bombs.

The march came just several days after news broke of a massacre of South Vietnamese civilians by U.S. troops in South Vietnam. Americans learned that in March 1968, soldiers in the tiny village of My Lai had killed several hundred people who had not attacked them, after which the Army tried to hide the incident. Some Americans refused to believe that U.S. troops would do such a thing. To those who opposed the war, the massacre was another reason the United States should get out of Vietnam.

Despite the news of My Lai and the Washington march, the antiwar movement seemed quiet for a time. There were rallies on some college campuses on April 15, 1970, but they were small compared with some in the past. The quiet, though, would shatter after the 13 seconds of shooting at Kent State.

NIXON AND THE PROTESTERS

President Richard Nixon talked to protesters near the White House after the Kent State shootings.

President Richard Nixon tried to act as if November 15, 1969, was just another day. He made a point of telling the news media that he would be home at the White House watching football. But Nixon worried that the protest would become violent. He had several hundred specially trained soldiers stationed in hiding places near the White House, and a ring of buses blocked access to the building from the street.

As president, Nixon had his first direct contact with antiwar protesters on his first day in office. During his inaugural parade on January 20, 1969, some protesters threw rocks at his limousine and chanted antiwar slogans. But his most famous encounter with antiwar protesters was after the Kent State shootings.

He went out late one night to talk to protesters near the Lincoln Memorial. Most people who heard the conversation thought Nixon had not always made sense that night. One protester later said, "I hope it was because he was tired but most of what he was saying was absurd." Another protester said the president had mumbled and hadn't looked them in the eye. Nixon, though, thought he had expressed important points clearly. One thing he said about Vietnam, he later recalled, was "I hope that [your] hatred of the war, which I could well understand, would not turn into a bitter hatred of our whole system, our country and everything that it stood for."

ChapterThree
THE NATION REACTS

During the rally of May 4, several Kent State students tried to document what was happening. In his dorm room, Terry Strubbe turned on a tape recorder that captured the sound of chanting students, the shouts of guardsmen, and the firing of their guns. Other students grabbed their cameras and took pictures. One of them was John Filo. He had missed the weekend protests and violence on campus because he had left Kent to work on his senior project. Filo was disappointed when he returned to the university on Sunday and learned what had happened. He later said, "It was the biggest news event of my life and I had missed it. I was extremely depressed."

But on May 4, as he set out for lunch with his camera and saw the scene on the Commons, Filo gave himself a goal. He wanted to "make a photo that represented what was going on in the nation with the students and their protests against the war in Vietnam." He soon captured protester Alan Canfora waving a black flag as he stood in front of the guardsmen. Filo later called it "my best photo ever." But soon he would take an even better photo, one of the most famous of the Vietnam era—and one that met the goal he had set for himself.

John Filo called his May 4 picture of Alan Canfora waving a black flag in protest his "best photo ever."

A few minutes later, Filo heard the guardsmen open fire. He, like most of the students on the Commons, thought the soldiers were firing blanks. Filo was shocked when a guardsman aimed a rifle at him and fired. The bullet created a cloud of dust as it hit a nearby statue. He dropped his camera, then quickly checked himself to make sure he wasn't hit. While other students dived for cover, Filo retrieved his camera and then scanned the scene. He saw student Jeffrey Miller lying face down, with blood running onto the pavement. Miller had recently transferred to the university from Michigan State

University. He had opposed the Vietnam War since high school and had taken part in the Sunday night protest. The morning of May 4, he called his mother and told her he was attending another rally. "Don't worry, Mom," he said. "I may get arrested, but I won't get my head busted."

Seeing Miller on the ground, Filo started to run, but then he caught himself, thinking, "Where are you going? This is why you are here!" He walked toward Miller and began taking pictures. People approached Miller's fallen body. One of them was Mary Ann Vecchio, a 14-year-old runaway from Florida who was on campus for the protests. As Filo later described it, "I could see the emotion welling up inside of her. She began to sob. And it culminated in her saying an exclamation. I can't remember what she said exactly … something like, 'Oh, my God!'" The picture he took in that instant came to sum up many of the feelings the nation had about the Vietnam War. Filo's picture shows Vecchio letting out her cry of despair as she crouches over Miller's motionless body. She later said she had been calling for help because she had felt helpless to do anything herself.

When he finished shooting six rolls of film, Filo drove for about two hours to a Pennsylvania newspaper where he sometimes worked. There he developed the film and began feeding the photos into the electrical network used to transfer photos

"I could see the emotion welling up inside of her. She began to sob."

John Filo was a 22-year-old student when he took the photo that would bring the Vietnam War home to America.

before the age of digital cameras. The photos would be sent across the country by the Associated Press, which provides news stories and photos to many newspapers. The first picture to reach the AP showed Vecchio over Miller's body. While other newspaper photographers had shot pictures of the mass of guardsmen and the clouds of tear gas, Filo's picture captured the true story of the day—the killing of four students and wounding of nine others on a college campus.

The image that appeared in newspapers, and on the cover of *Newsweek* magazine, was cropped—some of the left part of the frame had been cut out, to remove an object lying near Miller's head. The crop also took out empty space in the foreground, bringing Miller and Vecchio closer to the viewer and adding to the image's impact. A later version of the picture was altered to remove a post in the background that was directly above Vecchio's head. But the cropping did not alter the importance of the photo. The next year, Filo won the highest award in journalism, a Pulitzer Prize, for his distinguished spot news photo. To some people, the picture showed the power of the government over the protesters. Others saw it as an example of how the Vietnam War affected people thousands of miles away from the fighting.

When the shooting stopped that day at Kent State, students soon heard about the dead and wounded. Also killed were Allison Krause, Bill Schroeder, and Sandra Scheuer. Krause, 19, had been at the rally the night before. Earlier that day she had talked with a guardsman

Jeffrey Miller, Allison Krause

who had a flower in the barrel of his gun, placed there by a protester. When an officer ordered the soldier to remove it, Krause had said, "What's the matter with peace? Flowers are better than bullets." On Monday, she and her boyfriend came out to protest. When the firing started, they ducked behind a car, but a bullet still found Krause.

Schroeder, 19, was in ROTC on campus, but he had begun to oppose the Vietnam War. After going to a class on Monday, he was on the fringes of the protest but did not take part in it. He was in the same parking lot as Krause when he got hit. He died from his wound soon after being taken to the hospital.

Bill Schroeder, Sandra Scheuer

Sandra Scheuer, 20, was also hit in the parking lot. An honors student, she had not taken part in any of

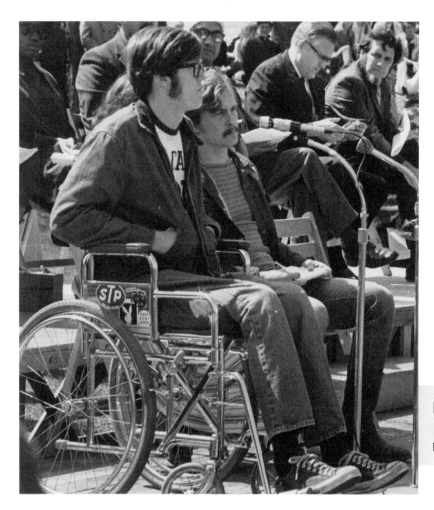

Dean Kahler (front) would never walk again.

the protests. She was merely walking across campus when a bullet hit her in the neck.

Dean Kahler, a 20-year-old student, was shot in the back and was paralyzed from the chest down. He uses a wheelchair today. Another victim, Joseph Lewis, 18, nearly died after bullets tore through his side. The other students wounded were Alan Canfora, John Cleary, Thomas Grace, Donald Scott MacKenzie, James Russell, Robert Stamps, and Douglas Wrentmore.

After the firing stopped, the guardsmen retreated to the burned-out ROTC building. Students came to

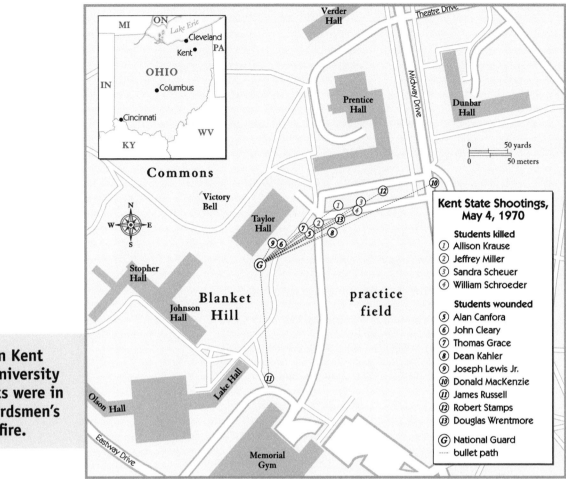

Kent State Shootings, May 4, 1970

Students killed
1. Allison Krause
2. Jeffrey Miller
3. Sandra Scheuer
4. William Schroeder

Students wounded
5. Alan Canfora
6. John Cleary
7. Thomas Grace
8. Dean Kahler
9. Joseph Lewis Jr.
10. Donald MacKenzie
11. James Russell
12. Robert Stamps
13. Douglas Wrentmore

G. National Guard
---- bullet path

Thirteen Kent State University students were in the guardsmen's line of fire.

help their fallen classmates, calling for ambulances or trying to help the wounded. After the dead and wounded were taken away, several hundred students still stood around the Victory Bell, while guardsmen also remained on the Commons. Several faculty members talked to students and to General Canterbury, trying to prevent more bloodshed. One of the professors, Glenn Frank, said to the students, "I am begging you right now. If you don't disperse right now, they're going to move in, and it can only be a slaughter." Finally, by 1:30 p.m., the students had pulled back, and Kent State's president soon closed the school.

The Kent State killings, especially as symbolized by John Filo's photo, stunned the nation. To those who opposed the Vietnam War, the killings were just another reason to end the war as soon as possible. The U.S. Congress soon began the slow process of cutting funding for the war. It also added a section to a revised Voting Rights Act that lowered the voting age to 18. For several years, young Americans had argued that if people under 21 were old enough to die in Vietnam, they were old enough to vote. Congress strengthened the voting law by passing an amendment to the Constitution that was quickly ratified by the states and confirmed the new voting age.

Some Americans, however, blamed the students for the killings. If they hadn't protested, their view went, the National Guard wouldn't have been on campus. A survey of Americans in mid-May found that 58 percent of them blamed the students for what had happened on May 4. Some people even said the guardsmen should have killed more students. A Kent resident said, "My own gas station man said they should have shot 100 of them." That attitude was voiced across the country by Americans who were tired of the years of protests by students and radicals. The feeling was expressed in some of the letters the parents of Bill Schroeder received.

The Kent State killings, especially as symbolized by John Filo's photo, stunned the nation.

PROTESTING IN SONG

Neil Young (from left), David Crosby, Graham Nash, and Stephen Stills protested the killings with "Ohio."

Songs protesting injustice and war have a long tradition in the United States, with roots in folk music and the blues. During the 1960s Bob Dylan helped bring the tradition to a wider audience, as did later rock musicians, often focusing on the Vietnam War. One example of the protest music was "Give Peace a Chance," recorded in 1969 by John Lennon of the Beatles.

After the Kent State killings, Neil Young saw an issue of *Life* magazine with photos taken on May 4. The issue did not have John Filo's famous image, but others he took appeared. Young was moved by the killings. The guitarist and songwriter quickly wrote the song "Ohio" to describe the day's events and the horror they inspired. The lyrics include the lines, "Tin soldiers and Nixon coming, We're finally on our own. This summer I hear the drumming, Four dead in Ohio."

Young recorded the song with his bandmates David Crosby, Stephen Stills, and Graham Nash. Some radio stations would not play it, but millions of Americans still heard the song condemning the violence at Kent State.

"There's nothing better than a dead destructive, riot making communist," one letter writer said, "and that's what your son was, if not he would have stayed away like a good American would do." The letter writer continued, "They should all be shot, then we'd have a better U.S.A. to live in." John Filo heard comments like that too. He received hate mail after his photo was published, and his own uncle said to him, "If you were out there, you should have been shot."

The most visible reaction to the killings came on college campuses across the United States. First thousands and then tens of thousands of students began to protest the killings and refused to attend classes. By one estimate, 4 million students on 850 campuses eventually took part. Protests of some kind occurred on about 80 percent of the country's campuses. The protests spread to some high schools as well, and demonstrators around the world protested both the killings and the Cambodia invasion. On May 9, about 100,000 protesters came to Washington, D.C. Once again, President Nixon remained in the White House, with extra security protecting the building.

At Jackson State College, a historically black school in Jackson, Mississippi, students came out for two nights of protests. The protesters were angry about the Kent State shootings, the war, and the treatment of blacks in the United States. By May 14, the protests in Jackson had turned confrontational,

Bullets riddled a dorm behind Jackson State students who gave the black power salute after attending a memorial service for the two young men killed by police.

and a rumor that a Mississippi civil rights leader had been killed led to violence. Police officers fired into a crowd, killing one Jackson State student and a local high school student and injuring a dozen others. The incident touched on two of the great issues of the era—the Vietnam War and the status of blacks in the United States. The Jackson State killings, however, did not receive as much attention as those at Kent State.

At first, President Nixon and other government officials did not seem to show much sympathy for

Boston demonstrators were among the millions of college students across the country who protested the Kent State killings.

the Kent State protesters. In his first statement, the president called the killings "tragic" and "unfortunate," but he seemed to suggest that the protesters had caused it with their violence. During a May 8 news conference, Nixon was reminded that just a few days before May 4, he had called student protesters "bums." During the news conference he said he had meant only those who caused violence. After the nationwide student protest, though, Nixon realized he needed to do more about both Kent State and Jackson State. People wanted to know why the students were killed and who was responsible. In June Nixon established the President's Commission on Campus Unrest. It's often called the Scranton Commission after its leader, former Pennsylvania governor William Scranton.

After months of investigation, the commission drew several conclusions about the events at Kent State. About the students, the commission said, "The widespread student opposition to the Cambodian action and their general resentment of the National Guardsmen's presence on the campus cannot justify the violent and irresponsible actions of many students during the long weekend. … For students deeply opposed to the war, the Guard was a living symbol of the military system they opposed. For other students, the Guard was an outsider on their campus, prohibiting all their rallies, even peaceful ones, ordering them about, and tear gassing them when they refused to obey."

Still, the commission found, the students' actions and attitudes did not justify what happened: "The indiscriminate firing of rifles into a crowd of students and the deaths that followed were unnecessary, unwarranted, and inexcusable." The Scranton Commission couldn't explain why the guardsmen had bullets in their guns or why they fired. The unanswered questions angered people both on and off the Kent State campus.

ChapterFour
LOOKING FOR ANSWERS

The Scranton Commission represented the first major effort to find out what really happened at Kent State on May 4, 1970. Much of the commission's information came from an investigation done by the Federal Bureau of Investigation (FBI) shortly after the killings. It showed that reports that the National Guardsmen faced direct threats and sniper fire and feared for their lives were untrue. Several guardsmen contradicted those who made the claims, and one said that after the killing some guardsmen created a story of being threatened as an excuse for the shooting.

Another step in trying to establish the truth came through the court system. The governor called for a special grand jury to consider whether anyone had committed a crime in the May 4 incident. In October a state grand jury recommended charging 25 people with crimes—none of them guardsmen. The troops, the jury's report said, "fired their weapons in the honest and sincere belief … that they would suffer serious bodily injury had they not done so." The grand jury concluded that they had not committed a crime. The jury also blamed Kent State officials for making it more important to protect the students' right to protest than to keep order on campus. The trials for the 25 began in the fall of 1971. One person

Kent State students protested the trial of the 25 people charged after the May 4 incident. The charges were in connection with the burned ROTC building and not the killing of the four students.

was acquitted, one was found guilty, two pleaded guilty to lesser charges, and the charges against the rest were dismissed.

Some defenders of the students called for the U.S. government to investigate using a federal grand jury. The survivors of the shooting, the families of the dead, and their supporters wanted the guardsmen charged for their actions. The federal government finally called a grand jury in 1973. The jury indicted eight of the guardsmen. While some people applauded the move, others thought National Guard

officers on the scene and even Governor Rhodes should have faced trial too. At the trial for the eight guardsmen, the judge ruled that the government had not proved their guilt. So they received no punishment from the courts for the shootings.

The trial took place in November 1974, and the situation in the United States was much different than it had been in May 1970. Richard Nixon had won re-election in 1972, but he was now under investigation. The Watergate hearings considered whether Nixon and his staff had covered up crimes committed during the election campaign. Nixon

Most of the National Guardsmen were not charged after the Kent State shootings.

faced a legal process called impeachment, which could have removed him from office. Rather than risk impeachment, Nixon resigned as president in August 1974. Four years later a former Nixon aide wrote that Kent State had played a part in the president's downfall. Nixon had become obsessed with confronting people he saw as enemies, even if it meant breaking the law.

Before he resigned, Nixon finally carried out his promise to remove U.S. troops from Vietnam. By the end of 1973, only a small force remained in the South Vietnamese capital of Saigon. North and South Vietnamese troops continued to battle, however, until the north finally won the war in April 1975. Vietnam was once again a single country, now under communist rule.

The war was over, but for Americans it was still a source of anger and conflict. Opponents remained convinced that the country should not have sent so many soldiers to die in a war that had little direct impact on the United States. More than 58,000 Americans died in Vietnam—along with about 1.3 million Vietnamese soldiers on both sides, and an unknown number of civilians. More than 300,000 Americans were wounded during the war. Some U.S. military officials thought the country's political leaders hadn't let them do enough to attack North Vietnam directly and perhaps force the north to end

the war sooner. The war created divisions among some Americans that lasted for years.

The federal trial of the National Guardsmen in November 1974 once again left the families and survivors of the killings angry. The next year they brought a civil case in federal court. They had started the process right after the shootings, but they had been required to go through a long legal battle to finally have their day in court.

The early trials had been criminal cases—the government had been trying to determine whether someone had broken a criminal law. Civil cases often

The actions of the National Guardsmen on the Kent State University campus would be the subject of several trials through the years.

involve legal disputes between individual people or groups of them, with one side trying to force an action or get money from the other. The Kent State victims and their families sued Governor Rhodes, individual guardsmen, former university president Robert White, and several others.

The trial lasted 15 weeks, and the judge called it one of the most complex civil cases ever. Court records of the witnesses' testimony filled almost 13,000 pages. The attorney for the students, Joseph Kelner, reminded the jury that Governor Rhodes had said the "National Guard should use whatever force was necessary" to disperse student rallies and meetings at Kent State. No one would go to jail for what happened on May 4, Kelner said, but the victims and the relatives wanted someone to take responsibility for what happened. In the end, though, the jury sided with Rhodes, the guardsmen, and the other defendants. None of them received any legal blame for what happened at Kent State.

Angered with this verdict, the victims and families continued their legal battle. They filed an appeal in 1976 and the next year won the right to have another trial. In January 1979 the state of Ohio agreed to settle the case for $675,000—much less than what the victims had sought. About half of the money went to Dean Kahler, the student who had been partly paralyzed by the shootings.

Elaine Holstein, the mother of Jeffrey Miller, said she and other parents and victims felt pressure from the judge and their lawyers to accept the settlement. But to her, the case was not about the money.

"I wanted an assurance," she said, "that no mother would ever again have to bury a child for simply exercising the freedom of speech. But all we got was a watered down statement that better ways must be found, etc., etc."

Rhodes and others who were sued issued a statement saying, in part: "In retrospect the tragedy of May 4, 1970, should not have occurred. … We deeply regret those events and are profoundly saddened by the deaths of four students and the wounding of nine others. … Some of the guardsmen … fearful and anxious from prior events, may have believed in their own minds that their lives were in danger. Hindsight suggests another method would have resolved the confrontation."

Since the 1979 settlement, some of the surviving shooting victims have continued to seek answers about what happened on May 4, 1970. They want to know why the guardsmen fired and whether they received an order to fire. It seems unlikely that a group of soldiers would have turned at the same time and fired if the action had not been planned.

Evidence that there was such an order seemed to emerge in 2010, when new digital technology was used to enhance sounds on the Terry Strubbe tape.

It seems unlikely that a group of soldiers would have turned at the same time and fired if the action had not been planned.

CONTINUING THE WORK

National Guardsmen turned as one and opened fire on Kent State students at 12:24 p.m. on May 4, 1970.

"This is an outrage!" said Alan Canfora in the courtroom when he heard that the jury in the civil trial had sided with Governer Rhodes and the other defendants. That outrage and the sense that justice had not been served led Canfora to spend nearly 50 years trying to find out what happened on May 4, 1970. Canfora was actively involved in protesting both the Vietnam War and the National Guard's presence at Kent State. He had belonged to Students for a Democratic Society, though the national group had disbanded the year before. When the shooting started, he said he could not believe that the guardsmen were firing real bullets—until one pierced his wrist. When the shooting stopped, he ran through the parking lot and saw students on the ground, including Jeffrey Miller. "I thought people were just injured," he said.

At the hospital, he said, "it was a totally chaotic, bloody scene." He heard about three of the deaths and then learned that Bill Schroeder had been talking to the doctors there just before he died. In the years after, Canfora said, he had trusted others to write the real history of the Kent State killings, but he had realized he had a part to play in that process. The mission became more urgent in 1988, the year that Arthur Krause, the father of Allison Krause, died. He had been a key figure in bringing the lawsuits and pursuing the truth. Canfora said he saw Krause before his death, and had promised him that he would "continue his work and seek truth and justice ... for the sake of those parents and for the other wounded students."

Three years before, Alan Canfora had found a long-forgotten cassette tape copy of the original recording that had been stored at Yale University. Two sound experts said they could hear someone giving an order to fire just before the shootings began. Canfora gave the tape to the U.S. Department of Justice in 2010 and asked government lawyers to review it. That would be the first step, Canfora hoped, in launching a new investigation of the killing. Two years later, however, the Justice Department decided not to reopen the case.

The survivors and their supporters have also struggled to get Kent State officials to honor the dead. In 1977 the college administration wanted

Parents of two of the slain students, Martin and Sarah Scheuer (left), and Arthur Krause, thanked folk singer Joan Baez, who appeared at a rally on campus. They protested in vain the building of a gym where their children had died.

IN LIVING MEMORY
OF
ALLISON KRAUSE
JEFFREY MILLER
SANDRA SCHEUER
WILLIAM SCHROEDER
MAY 4, 1970

DEDICATED MAY 4, 1971
BY BNAI BRITH HILLEL

REDEDICATED MAY 4, 1975

Mourners have placed stones on the top of one of the memorials to the slain students on the Kent State University campus.

to expand its gym onto part of the area where the shooting occurred. Students protested the decision, but the new building still went up. By then, Kent State students and several survivors of the shooting had started the May 4 Task Force. Its goal was to seek the truth about the shootings and to make sure that neither the college nor the country forgets what happened on that day. The task force is still active.

A memorial to the students killed and wounded was dedicated in 1990, 20 years after the shootings. A plaque lists their names. Engraved on the plaza's granite floor are the words "Inquire, Learn, Reflect."

The memorial is surrounded by 58,175 daffodils, the number of Americans killed in Vietnam. In 1999 the university put up markers—three in a parking lot and one nearby—on the spots where the students who died had been shot. The May 4 Visitors Center opened in 2014, to offer a history of the events of May 4. Visitors can take a walking tour that highlights important locations. The part of the campus where the shootings occurred has been added to the National Register of Historic Places.

When an anniversary of the May 4 shooting comes around, John Filo's famous photo is often shown. Decades later, it reminds Americans of both the horrors of that day and the way the war affected Americans. For Mary Ann Vecchio, the shooting was something she first wanted to forget. "It was such a horrific event," she said. "I felt guilty and shamed and hurt and I felt bad for the parents." Years later, she had come to accept her role in the history of the Vietnam War. "Years go by," she said, "and I am much better able to reflect more clearly on what happened."

Vecchio and Filo didn't meet until 1995, and the first time they appeared together at Kent State was in 2009. By then, Vecchio was a respiratory therapist. Filo had pursued his dream of becoming a photojournalist and had worked for several national news organizations. For years, Filo said, he had been afraid to talk to Vecchio. "I thought I had

Award-winning photographer John Filo with his famous photo that caught the anguish of the Kent State shootings

ruined her life," he said. The first time they met, they hugged. Filo is often asked about his photo. He said on the 30th anniversary of the shooting that "as a photographer, it is nice to know that there is a photo that you have taken that will live a little longer than you will."

When asked about the objectivity of journalists, Filo said that "a photo is never objective. If it is, it is real boring. It is the nature of freezing a moment. … That is the job of the photographer—simplify all that visual space, and put a frame around all that space, and say: 'this is what is important.'"

Timeline

April 30, 1970

President Richard Nixon, who had been elected president in 1968 after promising to end the war in Vietnam, announces he is sending U.S. troops into Cambodia

May 1, 1970

Students at Kent State University protest the invasion of Cambodia

May 4, 1970

National Guardsmen fire on student protesters, killing four and wounding nine; John Filo takes his picture of Mary Ann Vecchio kneeling next to the dead body of Jeffrey Miller

May 5, 1970

Students across the country begin to strike to protest the shootings at Kent State

May 2, 1970

The National Guard comes to the Kent State campus; some protesters burn the school's ROTC building

May 3, 1970

Students and guardsmen clash on campus

May 14, 1970

Law enforcement officials kill two African-American students in Jackson, Mississippi

1971

Filo wins a Pulitzer Prize for his photo

Timeline

1973

The United States signs a cease-fire agreement with North Vietnam and removes almost all its troops from South Vietnam

November 1974

In a federal trial, eight National Guardsmen are found not guilty of committing a crime in the May 4 shootings

1999

Kent State University sets up memorials to the four dead students

2009

Mary Ann Vecchio and John Filo appeared together at a May 4 commemoration on campus; memorial events are held every year

1975

Survivors of the shooting and relatives of the dead victims lose a civil lawsuit against Ohio Governor James Rhodes, National Guardsmen, and others; the May 4 Task Force is formed to seek the truth about the shootings and remember the victims

1979

The state of Ohio reaches a settlement with survivors of the shooting and relatives of the dead victims

2012

The U.S. government decides not to start a new investigation of the shootings despite a tape recording found earlier that seems to indicate that the guardsmen were given an order to shoot

2014

Kent State opens a visitors center to explain the history of the shooting

Glossary

capitalism—economic system that allows people to freely create businesses and own as much property as they can afford

casualties—people killed, wounded, or missing in a battle or in a war

communism—system in which goods and property are owned by the government and shared in common; communist rulers limit personal freedoms to achieve their goals

crop—to cut out part of a photo

dissent—public opposition to government policies

draft—system that chooses people who are compelled by law to serve in the military

indict—formally charge with a crime

nightstick—police officer's club

National Guard—voluntary military organization with units in each state, usually under the control of the state's governor but available to the president in times of war or emergency

objective—not influenced by personal feelings or opinions in considering and representing facts

photojournalism—use of photography to capture events and persons in the news

radical—extreme compared with what most people think or do

sanctuaries—places of safety

Soviet Union—former federation in eastern Europe and northern Asia that included Russia and 14 other now-independent countries

Additional Resources

Further Reading

George, Enzo. *The Cold War.*
New York: Cavendish Square Publishing, 2016.

Rice, Earle, Jr. *The Vietnam War.*
Philadelphia: Mason Crest, 2016.

Spilsbury, Richard. *Who Protested Against the Vietnam War?* Chicago: Heinemann Library, 2014.

Internet Sites

Use FactHound to find Internet sites related to this book. All of the sites on FactHound have been researched by our staff.

Here's all you do:
Visit *www.facthound.com*
Type in this code: 9780756554248

Critical Thinking Using the Common Core

John Filo said a photographer tries to capture what's important in the space in front of him. What are the important points made in his photo of Mary Ann Vecchio kneeling next to Jeffrey Miller's body? (Integration of Knowledge and Ideas)

What statements made after the May 4 shootings showed that some Americans supported the National Guard and opposed the protesters at Kent State? (Key Ideas and Details)

The Scranton Report found that the use of violence against the protesters was "unnecessary … and inexcusable." How does that differ from what the special grand jury reported in October 1969? (Craft and Structure)

Source Notes

Page 6, line 8: Richard Nixon: Address to the Nation on the Situation in Southeast Asia. 30 April 1970. 15 May 2016. The American Presidency Project. http://www.presidency.ucsb.edu/ws/?pid=2490

Page 6, line 24: May 1, Students Bury the Constitution. Kent State University Libraries. 15 May 2016. http://www.library.kent.edu/special-collections-and-archives/may-1-students-bury-constitution

Page 8, line 4: Carole A. Barbato, Laura L. Davis, and Mark F. Seeman. *This We Know: A Chronology of the Shootings at Kent State, May 1970.* Kent, Ohio: The Kent State University Press, 2012, p. 3.

Page 12, line 17: Ibid., p. 6.

Page 13, line 1: Scott L. Bills, ed., *Kent State/May 4: Echoes Through a Decade.* Kent, Ohio: The Kent State University Press, 1982, p. 87.

Page 14, line 8: *This We Know: A Chronology of the Shootings at Kent State, May 1970*, p. 8.

Page 20, line 18: Dwight D. Eisenhower: The President's News Conference. 7 April 1954. 15 May 2016. The American Presidency Project. http://www.presidency.ucsb.edu/ws/?pid=10202

Page 23, line 10: Michael S. Foley. *Confronting the War Machine: Draft Resistance During the Vietnam War.* Chapel Hill: The University of North Carolina Press, 2003, p. 29.

Page 24, line 9: Jo Freeman. "Dr. King Marches Against the War in Viet Nam in Chicago, March 1967." 15 May 2016. Jo Freeman.com. http://www.uic.edu/orgs/cwluherstory/jofreeman/photos/KingAtChicago.html

Page 26, line 23: Richard Nixon: Address to the Nation on the War in Vietnam. 3 Nov. 1969. 15 May 2016. The American Presidency Project. http://www.presidency.ucsb.edu/ws/?pid=2303

Page 27, line 4: Ibid.

Page 28, line 8: Joan Herbers. "250,000 War Protesters Stage Peaceful Rally In Washington; Militants Stir Clashes Later." *The New York Times.* 16 Nov. 1969. 15 May 2016. http://www.nytimes.com/learning/general/onthisday/big/1115.html

Page 29, col.2, line 4: Tom McNichol. "I Am Not a Kook: Richard Nixon's Bizarre Visit to the Lincoln Memorial." *The Atlantic.* 14 Nov. 2011. 15 May 2016. http://www.theatlantic.com/politics/archive/2011/11/i-am-not-a-kook-richard-nixons-bizarre-visit-to-the-lincoln-memorial/248443/

Page 29, col.2, line 10: Ibid.

Page 30, line 12: Bill Lilley. "Pulitzer Winner John Filo, Photo's Subject, Reunited at Kent State." *Akron Beacon Journal.* 6 May 2009. 15 May 2016. https://nppa.org/news/784

Page 30, line 17: Ibid.

Page 30, line 22: Ibid.

Page 32, line 4: Elaine Holstein. "My Son Was Killed 30 Years Ago at Kent State." *The Progressive.* 17 April 2000. 15 May 2016. http://progressive.org/media_mpholstein042700

Page 32, line 8: "Photographer John Filo discusses his famous Kent State photograph and the events of May 4, 1970." CNN. 4 May 2000. 15 May 2016. http://www.cnn.com/chat/transcripts/2000/5/4/filo/

Page 32, line 14: Ibid.

Page 35, line 6: Peter Davies and the Board of Church and Society of the United Methodist Church. *The Truth About Kent State: A Challenge to the American Conscience.* New York: Farrar Straus Giroux, 1973, p. 23.

Page 37, line 9: *This We Know: A Chronology of the Shootings at Kent State, May 1970*, pp. 27 and 29.

Page 38, line 24: Jerry M. Flint. "Kent's Townspeople Back Guardsmen." *The New York Times.* 8 May 1970, p. 18.

Page 39, col. 2, line 4: Neil Young Lyrics–Ohio. AZ Lyrics. 15 May 2016. http://www.azlyrics.com/lyrics/neilyoung/ohio.html

Page 40, line 1: Bill Schroeder. May 4 Archives.org. 15 May 2016. http://www.may4archive.org/bill_schroeder.shtml

Page 40, line 8: "Pulitzer Winner John Filo, Photo's Subject, Reunited at Kent State."

Page 42, line 2: John Kifner. "4 Kent State Students Killed by Troops. *The New York Times.* 5 May 1970. 15 May 2016. http://www.nytimes.com/learning/general/onthisday/big/0504.html

Page 42, line 7: The President's News Conference. 8 May 8 1970. 15 May 2016. The American Presidency Project. http://www.presidency.ucsb.edu/ws/?pid=2496

Page 43, line 8: *The Report of the President's Commission on Campus Unrest.* Washington, D.C.: Government Printing Office, 1970, pp. 287-288. http://files.eric.ed.gov/fulltext/ED083899.pdf

Page 43, line 21: Ibid., p. 289.

Page 44, line 18: Margaret Ann Garmon. "Legal Cases Chronology May 5, 1970–January 4, 1979." Kent State University Libraries. 15 May 2016. http://www.library.kent.edu/legal-chronology-may-5-1970-january-4-1979

Page 49, line 12: Joseph Kelner and James Munves. *The Kent State Coverup.* New York: Harper & Row, 1980, p. 239.

Page 50, line 5: Bob Collins. "On Kent State Anniversary, an Email from a Mother." Minnesota Public Radio. 4 May 2015. 15 May 2016. http://blogs.mprnews.org/newscut/2015/05/on-kent-state-anniversary-an-email-from-a-mother/

Page 50, line 11: "Legal Cases Chronology May 5, 1970–January 4, 1979."

Page 51, line 1: *The Kent State Coverup*, p. 254.

Page 51, line 16: Phone interview with Alan Canfora. 3 Feb. 2016.

Page 51, col. 2, line 1: Ibid.

Page 51, col. 2, line 12: Ibid.

Page 54, line 16: Matt Bai. "25 Years after Kent State, Photographer, Subject Finally Meet." *The Boston Globe.* 24 April 1995, p. B4. 15 May 2016. http://www.may4archive.org/globe04-24-95.shtml

Page 54, line 20: "Pulitzer Winner John Filo, Photo's Subject, Reunited at Kent State."

Page 54, line 28: Ibid.

Page 55, line 3: "Photographer John Filo discusses His famous Kent State photograph and the events of May 4, 1970."

Select Bibliography

Adams, Noah. "Shots Still Reverberate For Survivors Of Kent State." NPR. 3 May 2010. 5 April 2016. http://www.npr.org/templates/story/story.php?storyId=126423778

The American Presidency Project. 15 May 2016. http://www.presidency.ucsb.edu/index.php

Anderson, David L., ed. *Shadow on the White House: Presidents and the Vietnam War, 1945–1975.* Lawrence: University Press of Kansas, 1993.

Bai, Matt. "25 Years after Kent State, Photographer, Subject Finally Meet." *The Boston Globe.* 24 April 1995, p. B4. 15 May 2016. http://www.may4archive.org/globe04-24-95.shtml

Barbato, Carole A., Laura L. Davis, and Mark F. Seeman. *This We Know: A Chronology of the Shootings at Kent State, May 1970.* Kent, Ohio: Kent State University Press, 2012.

Bennett, Kitty. "Where are they now? Kent State Shootings 40 Years Ago." AARP Bulletin. 4 May 2010. 5 April 2016. http://www.aarp.org/politics-society/history/info-05-2010/where_are_they_now_kent_state_shootings.html

Bill Schroeder. May 4 Archives.org. 15 May 2016. http://www.may4archive.org/bill_schroeder.shtml

Bills, Scott L., ed. *Kent State/May 4: Echoes Through a Decade.* Kent, Ohio: Kent State University Press, 1982.

Chronology of Events, May 1–4, 1970. KSU Libraries and Media Services May 4 Chronology. 15 May 2016. http://www.library.kent.edu/special-collections-and-archives/ksu-libraries-and-media-services-may-4-chronology

Collins, Bob. "On Kent State Anniversary, an Email from a Mother." Minnesota Public Radio. 4 May 2015. 15 May 2016. http://blogs.mprnews.org/newscut/2015/05/on-kent-state-anniversary-an-email-from-a-mother/

Davies, Peter, and the Board of Church and Society of the United Methodist Church. *The Truth About Kent State: A Challenge to the American Conscience.* New York: Farrar Straus Giroux, 1973.

Dean Kahler Shot at Kent State May 4, 1970. 4 May 2015. 25 April 2016. https://www.youtube.com/watch?v=UCAXjFnRwBs

Flint, Jerry M. "Kent's Townspeople Back Guardsmen." *The New York Times.* 8 May 1970, p. 18.

Foley, Michael S. *Confronting the War Machine: Draft Resistance During the Vietnam War.* Chapel Hill: The University of North Carolina Press, 2003.

Freeman, Jo. "Dr. King Marches Against the War in Viet Nam in Chicago, March 1967." 15 May 2016. Jo Freeman.com. http://www.uic.edu/orgs/cwluherstory/jofreeman/photos/KingAtChicago.html

Galloway, Joseph L. "Who Lost Vietnam?" *The New York Times.* 20 Sept. 1998. 15 May 2016. https://www.nytimes.com/books/98/09/20/reviews/980920.20gallowt.html

Garmon, Margaret Ann. "Legal Cases Chronology May 5, 1970–January 4, 1979." Kent State University Libraries. 15 May 2016. http://www.library.kent.edu/legal-chronology-may-5-1970-january-4-1979

Hayden, Tom. "Closure at Kent State?" *The Nation.* 15 May 2013. 15 May 2016. http://www.thenation.com/article/closure-kent-state

Hensley, Thomas, and Jerry M. Lewis. *Kent State and May 4th: A Social Science Perspective.* Dubuque, Iowa: Kendall/Hunt Publishing Company, 1978.

Herbers, Joan. "250,000 War Protesters Stage Peaceful Rally In Washington; Militants Stir Clashes Later." *The New York Times.* 16 Nov. 1969. 15 May 2016. http://www.nytimes.com/learning/general/onthisday/big/1115.html

Holstein, Elaine. "My Son Was Killed 30 Years Ago at Kent State." *The Progressive.* 17 April 2000. 15 May 2016. http://progressive.org/media_mpholstein042700

Isaacs, Jeremy, and Taylor Downing. *Cold War: An Illustrated History, 1945–1991.* Boston: Little, Brown & Company, 1998.

Karnow, Stanley. *Vietnam: A History.* New York: Viking, 1991.

Kelner, Joseph, and James Munves. *The Kent State Coverup.* New York: Harper & Row, 1980.

"Kent State Shooting Divided Campus and Country." NPR. 3 May 2010. 15 May 2016. http://www.npr.org/templates/story/story.php?storyId=126480349

Kent State Shootings: Digital Archives. Kent State University Libraries. http://omeka.library.kent.edu/special-collections/kent-state-shootings-digital-archive

Kifner, John. "4 Kent State Students Killed by Troops." *The New York Times.* 5 May 1970. 15 May 2016. http://www.nytimes.com/learning/general/onthisday/big/0504.html

Lewis, Jerry M., and Thomas R. Hensley. The May 4 Shootings at Kent State University: The Search for Historical Accuracy. 15 May 2016. http://www.kent.edu/may-4-historical-accuracy

Lilley, Bill. "Pulitzer Winner John Filo, Photo's Subject, Reunited at Kent State." *Akron Beacon Journal.* 6 May 2009. 15 May 2016. https://nppa.org/news/784

Mangels, John. "Justice Department won't reopen probe of 1970 Kent State shootings." *Cleveland Plain Dealer.* 24 April 2012. 15 May 2016. http://www.cleveland.com/science/index.ssf/2012/04/justice_department_wont_re-ope.html

Perlstein, Rick. *Nixonland: The Rise of a President and the Fracturing of America.* New York: Scribner, 2008.

"Photographer John Filo discusses his famous Kent State photograph and the events of May 4, 1970." CNN. 4 May 2000. 15 May 2016. http://www.cnn.com/chat/transcripts/2000/5/4/filo/

The Report of the President's Commission on Campus Unrest. Washington, D.C.: Government Printing Office, 1970. http://files.eric.ed.gov/fulltext/ED083899.pdf

Reporting Vietnam: American Journalism, 1959–1975. New York: The Library of America, 2000.

Summers, Harry G., Jr. *The Vietnam War Almanac.* New York: Facts on File, 1985.

Sheeran, Thomas J. The Associated Press. "Kent State Audio Tape Released." *The Washington Post.* 2 May 2007. 15 May 2016. http://www.washingtonpost.com/wp-dyn/content/article/2007/05/02/AR2007050200322.html

Vietnam Online. American Experience. PBS. 15 May 2016. http://www.pbs.org/wgbh/amex/vietnam/

Wyckoff, Whitney Blair. "Jackson State: A Tragedy Widely Forgotten." NPR. 3 May 2010. 5 April 2016. http://www.npr.org/templates/story/story.php?storyId=126423778

Young, Marilyn B. *The Vietnam Wars, 1945–1990.* New York: HarperCollins, 1991.

Index

About the Author

Michael Burgan has written many books for children and young adults during his 20 years as a freelance writer. Most of his books have focused on history. Burgan has won several awards for his writing. He lives in Santa Fe, New Mexico.